Glowing Animals

Rose Davidson

Washington, D.C.

How to Use This Book

Reading together is fun! When older and younger readers share the experience, it opens the door to new learning. As you read together, talk about what you learn.

YOU READ

This side is for a parent, older sibling, or older friend. Before reading each page, take a look at the words and pictures. Talk about what you see. Point out words that might be hard for the younger reader.

I READ

This side is for the younger reader.

As you read, look for the bolded words. Talk about them before you read. In each chapter, the bolded words are: Chapter 1: nouns • Chapter 2: action words • Chapter 3: places • Chapter 4: animal names

At the end of each chapter, do the activity together.

Table of Contents

Chapter 1: How Do Animals Glow? 4

Your Turn! 10

Chapter 2: Reasons to Glow 12

Your Turn! 22

Chapter 3: Places to Glow 24

Your Turn! 34

Chapter 4: Deep-Sea Creatures 36

Your Turn! 46

CHAPTER 1
How Do Animals Glow?

It's nighttime and everything outside is dark. Then there is a flash of light! You see a firefly go by.

When some **animals** glow, they are like nature's night-lights. Other animals glow during the day. Glowing helps them all survive.

 Lots of different **animals** glow. Fish, bugs, and even snails glow.

European glowworm

Some animals glow by making their own **light**. It's like turning on a light switch inside their bodies.

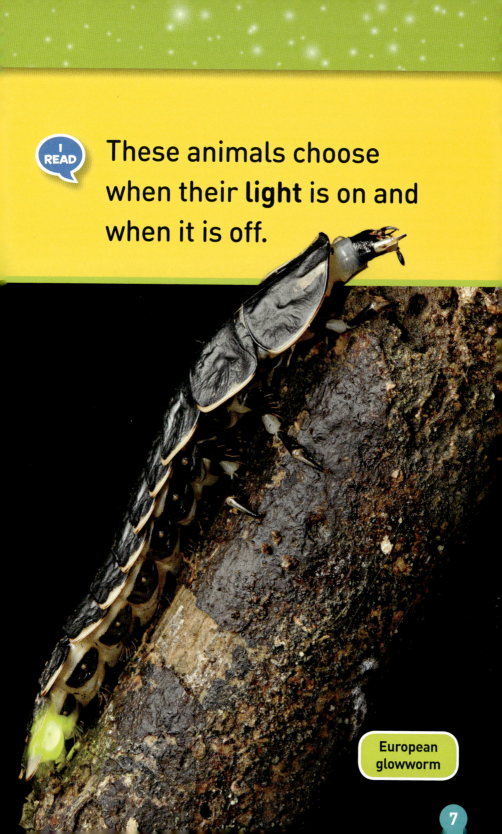

I READ These animals choose when their **light** is on and when it is off.

European glowworm

hawksbill sea turtle

Other animals need light from their surroundings to look a different **color**. First, the light hits their bodies. Then it's changed into different colors.

flower hat jellyfish

Their new **colors** could be colors like red, orange, yellow, green, or blue.

YOUR TURN!

Corals might not move, but they are animals, too. Look at these corals. Name the colors you see. Point to the colors on the pictures.

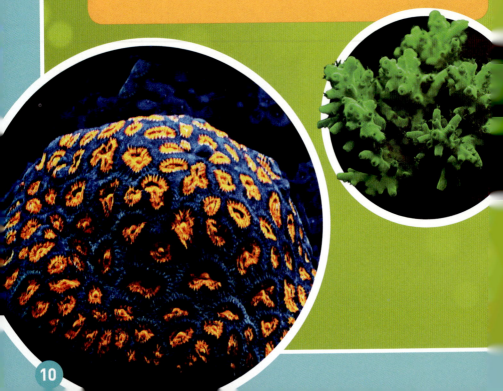

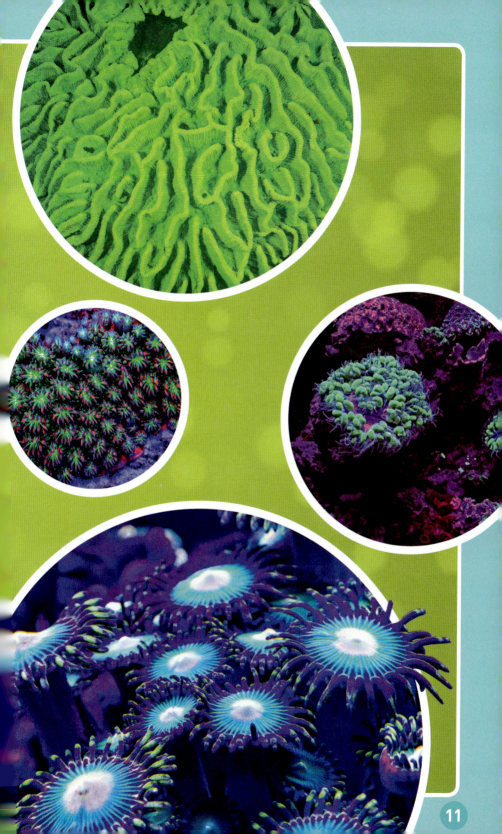

CHAPTER 2

Reasons to Glow

YOU READ

Animals have energy. They use it to move around, hunt, and stay alive. Some use it to make light, too. So why do animals glow? Different animals glow in different ways and for different reasons.

Fireflies glow to **attract** attention. Different fireflies flash at different times.

 A firefly's flashing light helps it **attract** and "talk" to other fireflies.

Creepy anglerfish wait patiently in the deep sea. They are ready to **lure** their next meal. Long, glowing skin dangles from the fish's head.

 To other animals, the light looks like a tasty worm. The light **lures** them to the fish's mouth.

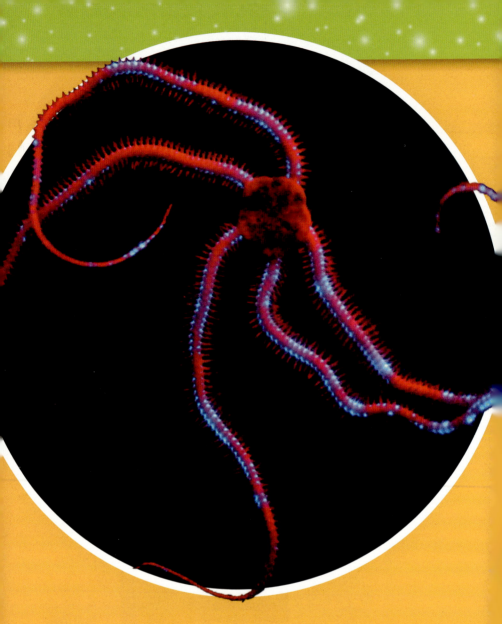

 Brittle stars are food for other animals. Their glow helps them **distract** hungry creatures. When a hungry creature is nearby, the brittle star removes a glowing arm.

The arm **distracts** the animal. Now the brittle star can crawl away.

pygmy shark

This tiny shark glows to **hide**! During the day or under the moonlight, its belly lights up. The color of its belly matches the light streaming down from above. Its belly blends into the light.

 Animals swim under the shark. They look up. They can't see the shark! It **hides** well.

With glowing green and red lights, a railroad worm looks like a tiny train. Green lights on its body look like windows. They **warn** animals that the worm tastes bad.

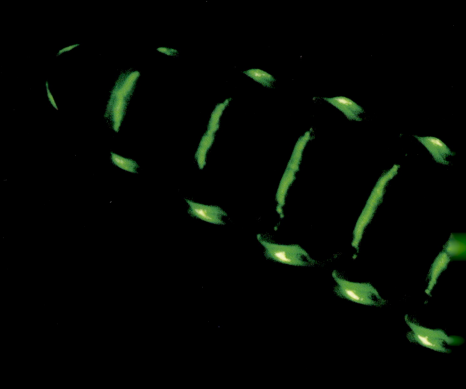

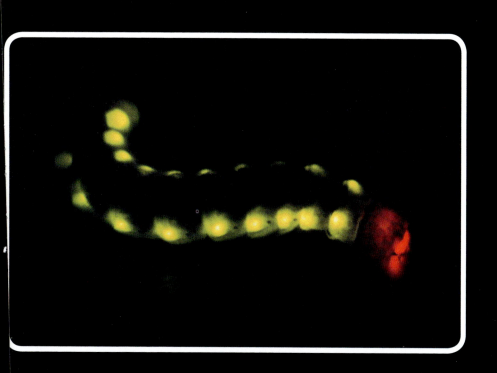

 The red lights don't **warn** animals. They help the worms see.

YOUR TURN!

Think about all the reasons animals glow. Then make up an imaginary animal and draw it. What color does your animal turn when it glows? Why does it glow?

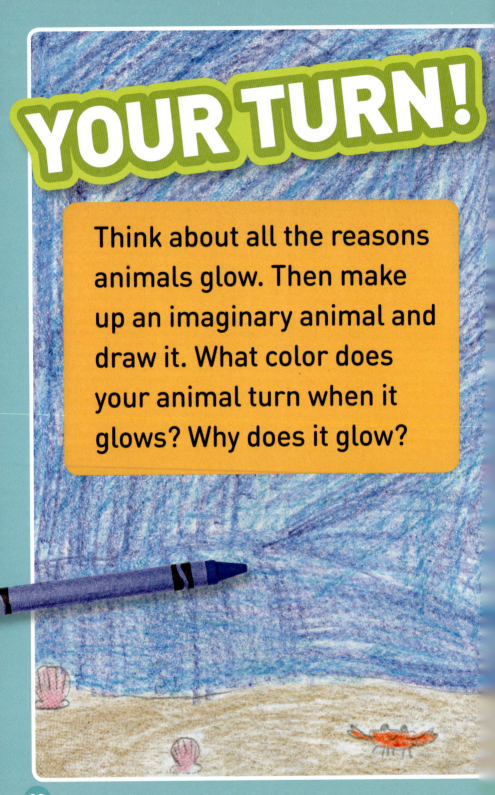

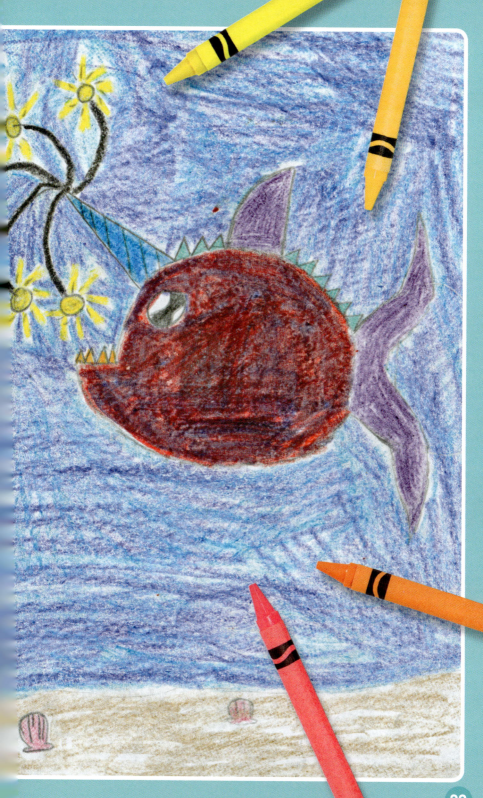

CHAPTER 3

Places to Glow

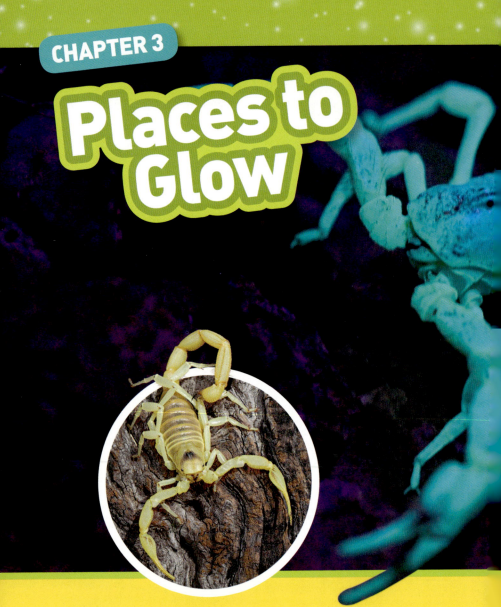

Animals that look glowing live in lots of places. In their hot, dry **desert** home, scorpions are active at night. Sometimes these scorpions look glow-in-the-dark, but scientists don't know why.

Some animals look like they "glow" when seen with a special kind of light called ultraviolet (or UV). This scorpion was photographed using a camera that captures UV light.

 Shining a special light on the scorpions helps people see their bright blue color in the dark **desert** night.

YOU READ

Underground, a damp, dark **cave** glitters with glowworms. They hang from the ceiling. Insects fly toward the glowing light.

The glowworms in the **cave** are covered in sticky goo. The insects get stuck. Then the glowworms eat the insects.

Polka-dot tree frogs hop from branch to branch in the **rainforest**. The rainforest is packed with colorful plants and animals. In the evening, the frogs look much brighter to other frogs.

Glowing might help these frogs find each other in the crowded **rainforest**.

This photo was taken with a camera that captures UV light.

In the big open **grassland**, there's a giant mound. Termites used to live here. Baby beetles, called larvae, live here now. At dusk, they twinkle to lure other bugs.

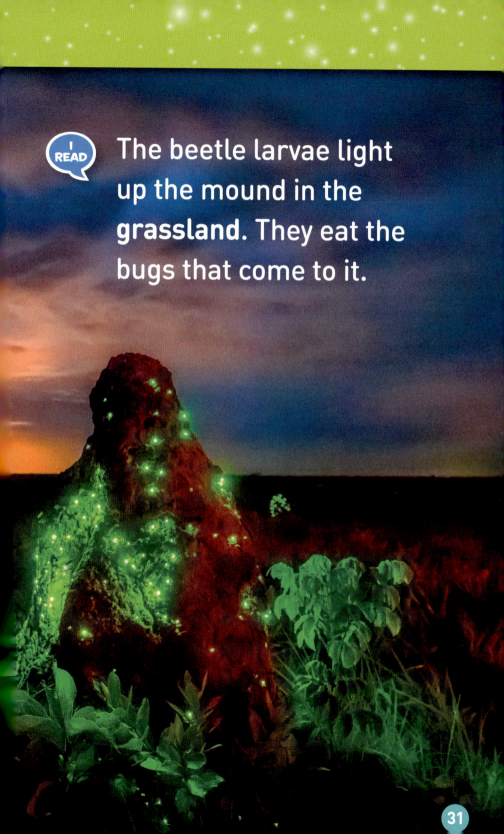

I READ

The beetle larvae light up the mound in the **grassland**. They eat the bugs that come to it.

The sun doesn't reach deep down in the **ocean**. So, animals bring their own light! More than three-fourths of all ocean animals glow. Squid, sharks, jellyfish, dragonfish, and other creatures all glow here.

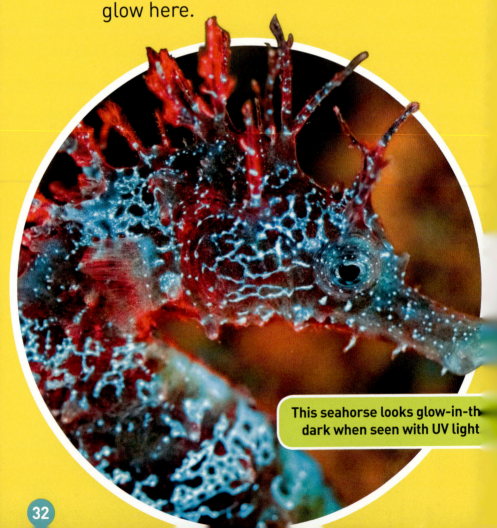

This seahorse looks glow-in-the dark when seen with UV light

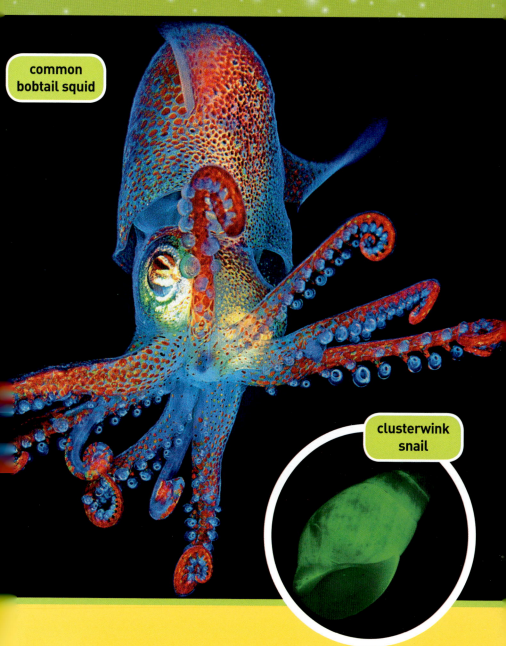

common bobtail squid

clusterwink snail

Most glowing animals on Earth live in the **ocean**.

33

YOUR TURN!

Look at each picture. Say the name of the place. Match the word to the correct picture.

1

Word Bank

desert
cave
rainforest
grassland
ocean

2

ANSWERS: 1. desert, 2. rainforest, 3. cave, 4. grassland, 5. ocean

35

CHAPTER 4
Deep-Sea Creatures

YOU READ

Firefly **squid** sparkle with so many tiny spots, they look like clusters of twinkling stars in the ocean. In the spring, the squid make their way from the deep sea to the shore.

I READ The glowing blue **squid** can be seen on the beach.

When this **jellyfish** is attacked, it flashes bright lights to find help. Bigger animals see the light and come toward the attacker.

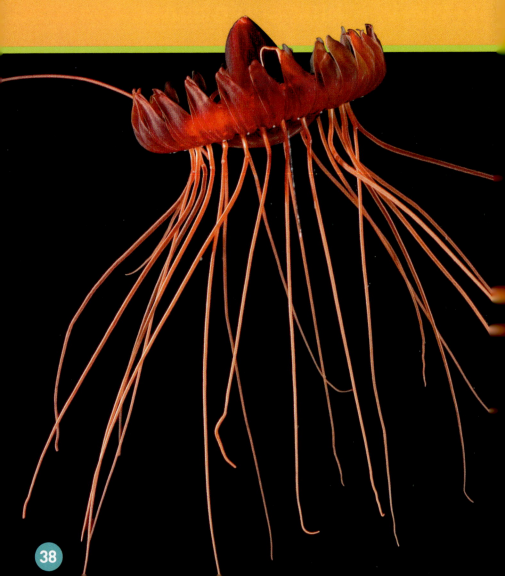

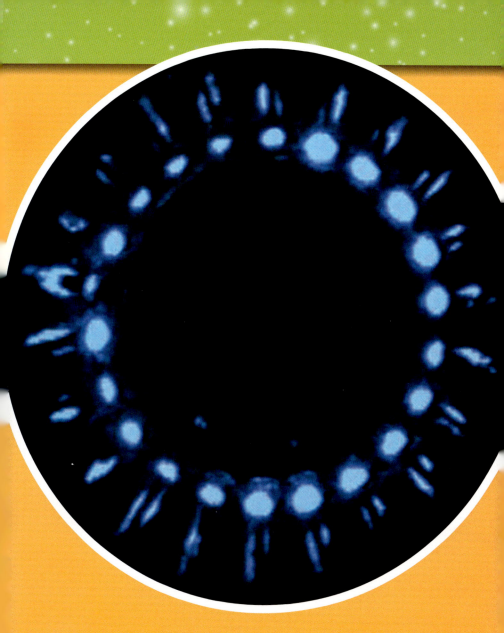

 This **jellyfish** has a nickname. It is called the "alarm jellyfish."

 This animal looks like a fish. But it's really a **sea slug**. The light of this slug is very bright, but people don't often see it.

These **sea slugs** are small. They are hard to find in the ocean.

 In the ocean, **bristle worms** are found everywhere. They come in a lot of shape and sizes. Some are 10 feet long. Some look like they glow.

This bearded bristle worm looks like it glows.

The scales are flat and hard. They keep the **bristle worms** safe.

Comb jellies flash light at deep-sea animals that want to eat them. They might do this to scare the other animals away. Comb jellies can sense light around them, too, even though they don't have eyes to see!

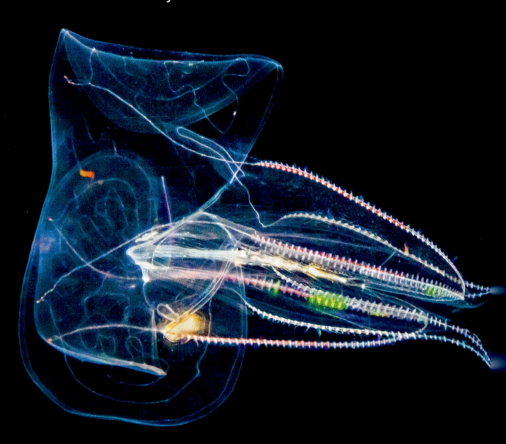

This swell shark and scorpion look like they glow.

 We still have a lot to learn about **comb jellies**, and other glowing animals, too!

ANSWERS: The glowing animals appear in pictures 3, 4, and 7.

47

For Bella —R.D.

Copyright © 2019 National Geographic Partners, LLC

All rights reserved. Reproduction in whole or in part without written permission of the publisher is prohibited.

NATIONAL GEOGRAPHIC and Yellow Border Design are trademarks of the National Geographic Society, used under license.

The author and publisher gratefully acknowledge the expert literacy review of Kimberly Gillow, principal, Chelsea District, Michigan, and the expert content review of David Gruber, National Geographic explorer, professor of biology, City University of New York, and research associate, invertebrate zoology, American Museum of Natural History.

Author's Note:
We talk about two kinds of "glowing" in this book: Bioluminescence (when an animal makes its own light, such as fireflies) and biofluorescence (when an animal appears "glow-in-the-dark" by taking in light of one color and re-emitting it as light of a different color). Biofluorescent animals don't really "glow" in the technical sense. They just appear so to humans, who can't see this light without the help of a UV light (on land) and a blue light (underwater). To animals that can see this light regularly, these animals look to be these glowing colors all the time!

Illustration Credits
GI: Getty Images; MP: Minden Pictures; NGIC: National Geographic Image Collection; SS: Shutterstock

Cover, kanyhun/Imazins/GI; border (throughout), mcherevan/SS; 1, Doug Perrine/SeaPics.com; 3, Fer Gregory/SS; 4–5, StagnantLife/GI; 6, Paul Hobson/NPL/MP; 7, Chien Lee/MP; 8–9, David Gruber; 9 (LO), Doug Perrine/NPL/MP; 10 (LE), Professor Joerg Wiedenmann, University of Southampton; 10 (RT), Gerald Nowak/SeaPics.com; 11 (UP), Stuart Westmorland/GI; 11 (CTR LE), Robin Westmorland/Danita Delimont/Gallo Images/GI; 11 (CTR RT), Donna O'Meara/NGIC; 11 (LO), D. R. Schrichte/SeaPics.com; 12 (LE), Atsuo Fujimaru/Nature Production/MP; 12 (RT), John Abbott/Nature Picture Library; 13, Cathy Keifer/SS; 14–15, Norbert Wu/MP; 16, Sonke Johnsen/Visuals Unlimited, Inc.; 17, Jon Kreider Underwater Collection/Alamy Stock Photo; 18–19, Doug Perrine/SeaPics.com; 19 (LO), Florian Graner/NPL/MP; 20–21, Danté Fenolio/Science Source; 21 (UP), Robert F. Sisson/NGIC/GI; 22–23 (crayons), Charles Brutlag/Dreamstime; 22–23 (drawing), Fiona Flynn; 24 (LO), Mark Kostich/GI; 24-25, Brian Green/Alamy Stock Photo; 26, CreativeMoments/GI; 27 (LE), Julian Money-Kyrle/Alamy Stock Photo; 27 (RT), Shaun Jeffers/SS; 28 (UP), Sam Spicer/SS; 28 (LO) and 29, Julian Faivovich and Carlos Taboada-Museo Argentino de Ciencias Naturales "Bernardino Rivadavia"; 30, Octavio Campos Salles/Alamy Stock Photo; 30-31, Marcio Cabral/Biosphoto/Alamy Stock Photo; 32, Raimundo Fernandez Diez/GI; 33 (UP), SeaTops/imageBROKER/SS; 33 (LO), © 2010 Dimitri Deheyn, Scripps Institution of Oceanography/UC San Diego; 34 (UP), Nenad Druzic/GI; 34 (LO), Sam Spicer/SS; 35 (UP LE), CreativeMoments/GI; 35 (UP RT), Octavio Campos Salles/Alamy Stock Photo; 35 (LO), Tobias Bernhard Raff/Biosphoto/MP; 36 (UP), David Liittschwager/NGIC/GI; 36 (LO), Solvin Zankl/MP; 37, Brian J. Skerry/NGIC/GI; 38, David Shale/NPL/MP; 39, Edith A. Widder, Operation Deep Scope 2005 Exploration, NOAA-OE; 40, Fabien Michenet; 41, Steven Kovacs/SeaPics.com; 42–43, Stuart Westmorland/Alamy Stock Photo; 43 (LO), Suzan Meldonian/Seapics.com; 44, Masa Ushioda/Seapics.com; 45 (UP), Scripps Institution of Oceanography/UC San Diego; 45 (LO), Brian Green/Alamy Stock Photo; 46 (UP LE), Krzysztof Odziome/SS; 46 (UP RT), Hanjo Hellmann/SS; 46 (LO), Edurivero/Dreamstime; 47 (UP), Marcio Cabral/Biosphoto/Alamy Stock Photo; 47 (CTR LE), Andrea Izzotti/SS; 47 (CTR RT), Sergey Lavrentev/SS; 47 (LO), Shaun Jeffers/SS

Library of Congress Cataloging-in-Publication Da

Names: Davidson, Rose, 1989- author. | National Geographic Society (U.S.)
Title: National geographic readers : glowing anima / by Rose Davidson.
Other titles: Glowing animals
Description: Washington, DC : National Geographi Kids, [2019] | Series: National Geographic readers | Audience: Age 4-6. | Audience: K to Grade 3. | Identifiers: LCCN 2018057542 (print) | LCCN 2018058838 (ebook) | ISBN 9781426335006 (e-book) | ISBN 9781426334986 (paperback) | IS 9781426334993 (hardcover)
Subjects: LCSH: Bioluminescence--Juvenile literature. | Animal behavior--Juvenile literature Classification: LCC QH641 (ebook) | LCC QH641 .D 2019 (print) | DDC 572/.4358--dc23
LC record available at https://lccn.loc.gov/2018057542

National Geographic supports K–12 educators with ELA Common Core Resources. Visit natgeoed.org/commoncore for more information.

Printed in the United States of America
21/WOR/3